CHRISTOPHER NOVAK

We've always done it that way.

"I'm not great at the advice. Can I
interest you in a sarcastic comment?"

Chandler, Friends

Contents

Foreword

In "We've always done it that way," Christopher Novak draws upon his extensive professional experience in marketing and communications to explore the concept of intrapreneurship. By presenting insights from his own journey, Novak outlines how embracing intrapreneurial qualities can lead to a more enriching and satisfying professional life for individuals across various fields.

Throughout this guide, Novak weaves personal anecdotes seamlessly with theories and concepts from the field, creating a holistic narrative that piques readers' interest. With each passage illuminated by both theoretical frameworks and real-world experiences, Novak provides a solid foundation from which readers can gain invaluable knowledge about embracing an intrapreneurial mindset.

Novak emphasizes that adopting an entrepreneurial approach within a corporate setting enables professionals to break free from stagnant routines and reimagine their work trajectories. By challenging traditional modes of operation and fostering innovation within existing structures, individuals become empowered agents capable of transforming their organizations positively. This shift not only facilitates career progression but also unlocks personal fulfillment as professionals harness their creativity while making substantial contributions within their respective roles.

What sets Novak's perspective apart is how he demonstrates that most people possess untapped potential for intrapreneurial growth regardless of position or industry. Through inspiring examples drawn across diverse sectors, he showcases success stories where individuals with varying backgrounds chose to embrace change over complacency. Moreover, Novak dismantles preconceived notions surrounding entrepreneurialism being solely associated with startups or entrepreneurship strictly tied to self-employment ventures; instead positioning invigorating forays into corporate environments actively engaging employees through opportunity-seeking behaviors necessary for staying agile amidst rapidly-changing market trends.

Ultimately, "We've always done it that way" serves as an indispensable resource for those seeking guidance in infusing entrepreneurial spirit into their professional lives. From industry veterans to recent graduates, Novak's forward-thinking insights illustrate the vast potential waiting to be unleashed within everyone willing to challenge tradition and embrace innovation for a more fulfilling career journey. By offering practical advice alongside captivating stories of intrapreneurial triumphs, he empowers readers with the tools required to navigate the shifting landscapes of today's workspaces while paving the way for future professional experiences that transcend convention.

Preface

Let's start with one of my go-to tales about who Christopher Novak is.

I woke up to the sound of my roommate, Mike, snore-choking himself awake. It was the first day of class at California University of Pennsylvania. Mike and I were both in quite a bit of pain from a long weekend of breaking in what we thought was the ideal college experience. As I got dressed for my first college class, I took out my phone to check on just how much damage I did to my bank account over the weekend. Damn.

It wasn't looking good. Day one of school and on the verge of bankruptcy. This immediate dread, combined with the jungle juice-induced headache I was experiencing began to weigh on me. I already had my reservations on my decision to study music at a state school in the Monongahela Valley, just south of Pittsburgh - but as I exited my dorm and lit my last cigarette, I called this choice into question even more heavily.

For the past ten years, I had studied music theory and every instrument I could afford to get my hands on. I wasn't a "band geek" though. Pshh, come on. Sure, I did join the school band my senior year of high school to ready myself for the world of higher education music theory. However, my real experience had come from countless weekends playing with my punk rock band in whatever "venue" of western Pennsylvania would have us. I played guitar, I sang lead vocals - whatever there was a need for, I would jump on the opportunity to try it out.

Now, I told myself I pursued those extracurricular activities to meet girls... But as those that have traveled a similar road know, I more often met like-minded dudes who just wanted to rock and share an exhilarating opportunity to act like our favorite rock stars.

As my thoughts wandered while walking to class, I thought "Is this really the life I want to live?" I mean, it's the second day on campus and I'm already broke and tired. Sure, the end goal wasn't to graduate with a degree to qualify my entry into a punk rock band, but rather something like 'music technology' or a similar field - which also is not famous for lavish incomes and public success stories.

I panicked and took a sharp right toward the admissions office. I had to figure this out. Maybe the kind and helpful folks at that admissions office (ha!) might have some guidance for me.

When I approached their bank teller-style desk, I stated my case and my reservations, ultimately ending my plea with, "Do you have anything else I can do here?"

"Well, is there anything you've been told you're particularly good at?" replied the assistant that was hearing me out.

Leveraging my innate sarcasm to try and defuse the lady at the admissions window, who was clearly annoyed by my request, and with a slick smile that I had been using my entire life in situations like this, I told her, "Actually, my mom always said I was full of shit. Have any degrees for that?"

It worked. She laughed briefly and began to gather some forms to hand me.
"We do. It's called Public Relations & Marketing."

I signed the course change forms and was on my way. I felt good about it. Exactly four years later, I was entering the workforce with the aforementioned degree and a strong desire to put my skills to the test.

Fast forward just six months and I came to the realization that this *work* thing isn't what I studied in school. Meetings. Meetings about meetings. And emails about the meetings about meetings. Even worse, the long hours and late nights spent perfecting the campaigns I was able to assist with never led to rewarding results. Just fire drills and lackluster enthusiasm from my more senior peers.

Where were the exciting campaigns I had conducted case studies on? Even if I could build something amazing, I found my impact and ability to shift the team toward a well-thought-through strategy was ineffective almost every time. I'll never forget the first time I called an illogical routine into question, immediately being met with a response that was burned into my psyche...

"That's the way we've always done it."

What I've written in this book is my solution to that and my advice to others who have been stifled by it.

Enjoy...
Christopher Novak

I

A how-to guide

*"Dare not choose in your minds the work you would
like to do when you leave the Home of the Students.
You shall do that which the Council of Vocations shall
prescribe for you."*
Ayn Rand, Anthem

1

What is Intrapreneurship?

Whether you are familiar with the term or not, the foundation of what you'll read in this book can be defined by a single personality archetype; **The Intrapreneur.**

I believe five distinct qualities help define an intrapreneur:

1. Driven: Someone who thinks like an intrapreneur is passionate about the workplace and desperate to make changes. He craves the positive gains from achieving success in the office, largely because he knows that they will have a personal, professional ripple effect on staff members. They will get better too.

2. Leader: An individual who can step outside of the regular confines of his position and bring a change to the industry is someone who knows how to lead. A good intrapreneur has a clear understanding of the benefits of efficiency and effectiveness.

3. Innovator: Being an intrapreneur is being a dreamer; someone who is unafraid of thinking big and develops strategies for tackling the way things have always been done, so that a bigger dollar amount lands on the bottom line at the end of the day.

4. Problem solver: Before asking someone to implement changes and fix a situation, an intrapreneur has to be able to recognize when something is dysfunctional. He must then quickly and succinctly develop a plan, implement *and cheer* as it all comes to fruition.

5. Risk taker: Comfort can set in when an employee has worked with the same company for several years and has seen colleagues and mentors retire with full benefits. The person who can break the mold and still see a bigger picture has the potential to be an intrapreneur.

It's easy to think of the intrapreneur as a "change-agent", always pushing other employees to be better and do better, but what's really behind the success of this player on the team is genuine care for the organization. An intrapreneur is someone who sees the organization as an opportunity for growth and applies entrepreneurial practices for the purpose of making something better for the organization. The person who takes an intrapreneurial approach is ambitious and driven, but also innovative, in the way that he tackles his workplace. He sees the goals of the company and his role in the context of the overall operation.

Being an intrapreneur in an organization that is stuck in its ways can present several challenges.

However, with the right mindset and approach, it is possible to navigate this situation effectively. Firstly, it is important to understand the reasons behind the organization being resistant to change. This could be due to various factors such as a rigid hierarchical structure or limited openness to new ideas.

To act as an intrapreneur, one must carefully observe these aspects and develop strategies accordingly. In addition, building strong relationships and alliances within the organization is crucial. By understanding who holds influence and engaging them in conversations about innovation and progress, you can start breaking down resistance barriers. These connections may also help generate support for your ideas among influential stakeholders.

Patience becomes imperative when dealing with a stagnant workplace culture. It may take time for your initiatives to gain traction or for others to see the value of embracing change. Being patient will allow you to consistently demonstrate commitment and perseverance while maintaining focus on your long-term goals.

Another strategy is finding small opportunities within existing processes where you can introduce innovative practices discreetly. By making incremental changes that deliver tangible results without disrupting overall operations significantly, colleagues might become more receptive towards larger-scale innovations over time.

In order not to appear confrontational or disruptive amidst resistance from traditional mindsets, effective communication becomes essential.

- **Utilize persuasive techniques** such as storytelling or providing case studies of successful implementations elsewhere that resonate with organizational values and objectives.
- **Taking ownership** of projects related to improving efficiency or addressing specific pain points can demonstrate entrepreneurial qualities even within a static environment.
- **Identifying areas where incremental improvements are needed** allows you not only create impact but also showcase adaptability without challenging deep-rooted systems directly.

A key aspect of acting as an intrapreneur is leading by example through continuous learning and personal growth. Constantly seeking out new skills, taking courses, and staying up-to-date with industry trends enables one to bring fresh perspectives to the organization, which can ultimately lead to greater acceptance of innovative approaches. Ultimately, being an intrapreneur in a stagnant organization requires finesse and carefully calculated strategies.

Understanding the reasons behind resistance, cultivating relationships, Patiently pushing for incremental changes, effective communication and leading by example are all valuable tools that can help you navigate these challenging situations successfully.

Of course, like the icons we think of in business, many people with the drive of the intrapreneur are attracted to opportunities granted to an entrepreneur, who sets forth on their own journey professionally. Entrepreneurs often struggle to thrive in large companies for several reasons.

The bureaucratic nature of these organizations inhibits their creativity and ability to take risks. In a rigid hierarchy where decision-making processes are slow and complicated, entrepreneurs may find themselves stifled by red tape.

The corporate environment tends to prioritize stability and conformity over innovation and disruption.

Established companies typically prefer incremental changes rather than disruptive ones that can significantly impact business operations. Consequently, entrepreneurs who thrive on pushing boundaries may find it challenging to work within this framework. Larger organizations tend to have established protocols and procedures that leave little room for individual autonomy or unconventional approaches - qualities essential for entrepreneurial success.

Another factor contributing to an entrepreneur's lack of success in large firms is resistance from peers or superiors who fear potential disruptions caused by innovative ideas or projects proposed by entrepreneurial individuals.

Traditional colleagues might view them as threats playing outside predefined company norms instead of recognizing their value as catalysts for growth. Testing new concepts quickly is crucial when pursuing entrepreneurial ventures; however, speed is not always prioritized within larger organizations due to factors such as risk-aversion and numerous internal approvals required before implementing changes.

While entrepreneurship facilitates tenacity amidst unknown landscapes without predetermined rules or guidelines; navigating structured environments wherein profits lie in maintaining stable foundations proves disconcerting for many innovators at heart – finding solace solely, oftentimes forcing the entrepreneurial spirit to seek other avenues tailored to their truest selves rather than compromise away from them.

2

Operating in a Silo

Once upon a time, in the bustling city of New York, there existed an advertising firm known as "Mad Ads Agency."

This extraordinary agency was home to some of the most creative minds and talented individuals in the industry. However, despite their immense potential, they faced a challenge that would put their skills and abilities to test – they did not communicate effectively while building campaigns.

In this particular story, Mad Ads Agency was assigned a high-stakes project for a renowned global brand. The client expected nothing short of brilliance from them. Yet sadly, within the walls of this prestigious agency, chaos ensued due to their poor communication habits.

There were multiple teams working on various aspects of the campaign simultaneously. Each team held different ideas and visions for how it should look and feel. Unfortunately, these differing perspectives were never communicated properly or reconciled effectively.

There was no centralized system to keep track of everyone's progress or update each other on individual contributions made towards the campaign. As a result, efforts were duplicated unnecessarily as one team unknowingly worked on what another had already completed diligently. Resources were spread thin and wasted in large amounts without anyone noticing until it was too late.

Due to incomplete information being circulated among team members at crucial junctures during decision-making processes; counterintuitive strategies started creeping into their masterpiece-in-the-making. The absence of clear communication channels led certain teams down misguided paths that strayed away from realizing the initial vision concurred upon with much excitement.

Consequently, long hours were spent fixing mistakes that could have been avoided if only better lines of communication had been established early on within this exceptional organization. Had each member taken note - collaborating readily across departments, - coordinating an effort with carefulness before beginning new endeavors, the desired outcome would have been achieved effortlessly as envisioned by all those passionate individuals breathing life into 'Mad Ads Agency.'

Sadly - the story of this renowned, fictional agency isn't hard to believe.

When teams in an organization "operate in a silo," it suggests that they work independently, with little communication or collaboration between them.

This metaphorical reference to a silo implies that each team functions within its own isolated space, unable or unwilling to share information, resources, or ideas with other teams.

Operating in a silo often leads to duplication of effort and wasted resources within the organization. Instead of capitalizing on collective knowledge and skills, each team focuses solely on its own objectives without considering the broader organizational goals. This lack of integration can hinder efficiency and innovation.

Operating in a silo can impede effective decision-making processes. Without cross-functional input and diverse perspectives from different teams working towards common objectives, decisions may become limited in scope and fail to consider all relevant factors. Silos also create barriers to effective communication across departments or units within an organization. Team members may not be aware of ongoing projects or initiatives outside their immediate focus area due to the lack of coordination among teams. Consequently, important information sharing is compromised.

Working within silos perpetuates competition rather than fostering cooperation between teams. Instead of collaborating for mutual success by leveraging interdisciplinary expertise and experiences, each team remains guarded about its achievements and innovations due to fear of losing prominence or recognition.

Breaking down these organizational silos becomes imperative for organizations seeking enhanced productivity and better outcomes. Encouraging greater inter-team collaboration through regular meetings, and shared databases/documentation systems could ensure an efficient flow of information which enables collective decision-making based on comprehensive insights. Besides facilitating formal channels for interaction between different functional units (such as cross-departmental task forces), cultivating a culture that promotes flexibility as well as recognizing individual contributions will play key roles too.

How can you beat the silo?

- Realigning performance measurement criteria so that they incentivize collaborative behavior can support breaking down existing barriers.
- Rotational programs/employee exchanges offering opportunities for employees from one department/team to experience the work environment and culture at another department would also provide a broader understanding of the organization and enhance collaboration.
- At the very least, make the role of "internal communication" someone's **job**. A newsletter or an intranet are good communication channels, but as with any goal, you need a strategy, content and **goals** - as well as the channel.

Moreover, an aspiring intrapreneur should identify ways to implement strategies that promote teamwork, integration, information sharing, and cross-functional cooperation which will be vital for breaking down these silos and fostering a more collaborative working environment.

3

Marketing to your own team

One of the early roles in my career was a *Corporate Communications* type assignment. As many in a corp-comm role will know, this job consisted of communicating changes in policy, organizational structure updates and informing the organization of all of the wins and losses.

As a twenty-something with a fancy new corporate gig, I was excited to talk about the job and share my life update - but I immediately found it hard to make the job sound *exciting*. I put my marketing hat on and invented a quick way to describe the role to someone that had never been exposed to organizations that had a department of that nature.

The moniker I came up with to describe the role in as few words as possible was "Internal Marketing".

It's what I used to describe it to my blue-collar friends, my dates, and even my 85-year-old grandmother. Hilariously, in overhearing my grandmother bragging to the other older

Italian ladies at church one Christmas, I heard her state, "Chris has a great job in propaganda." **I loved it** - it was basically spot-on. Sure... propaganda has a negative rhetorical sentiment associated with it, but it's accurate.

Separate the negative association of the word and the use of *propaganda* by government organizations to drive 'reefer madness' campaigns... and you have a team whose objective is to concentrate solely on **internal communication**.

Internal communication plays a crucial role in driving intrapreneurship within organizations. Effective and efficient communication channels enable employees to foster innovative ideas, collaborate with colleagues, and exhibit entrepreneurial behaviors. By creating an environment that encourages the sharing of knowledge and ideas, internal communication facilitates the development of intrapreneurial mindsets.

One way internal communication aids in promoting intrapreneurship is by providing a platform for idea generation. When employees are encouraged to share thoughts freely, they feel empowered to propose new concepts and solutions. Clear communication channels allow these ideas to be evaluated efficiently, enabling decision-makers to identify promising opportunities for further exploration.

Effective internal communication fosters collaboration among diverse teams within an organization. By facilitating open lines of dialogue between different departments or divisions, individuals are more likely to exchange knowledge and expertise. This inter-departmental collaboration engenders cross-pollination of ideas and increases the likelihood of intrapreneurial efforts gaining support from various stakeholders within the organization.

Establishing transparent information flows through effective internal communication helps ensure that all employees have access to vital business information necessary for making informed decisions aligned with organizational goals. When pertinent updates on market trends or industry insights are effectively communicated across all levels of hierarchy, employees become better equipped at identifying areas where innovation can occur within their specific roles.

Internal communication, or as my grandmother saw it, propaganda, plays a pivotal role in shaping corporate culture conducive to intrapreneurship. Companies that prioritize open dialogue and emphasize transparency will create an environment where risk-taking and creative thinking flourish naturally among their workforce. This cultural emphasis on intrapreneurship ultimately results in greater employee engagement as well as increased productivity levels company-wide.

Today, I see internal marketing as a key to driving pivotal culture change at any organization. I make it a habit to debrief with my team after a campaign concludes. It's just 'part of the process', the last leg of the campaign and the conclusion to any project I'm part of.

Looking busy can get you far in your career (I think many of us have worked with an 'empty suit' before). But when you begin to communicate your successes outwardly, share the hurdles you encountered and bond over common enemies and allies, you build a network and reputation for being results-oriented. This will inherently begin to motivate others around you to participate in sharing updates.

In short, one of the best ways I've found to ensure that I am always approaching the project of the day with a change management sensibility in tow is to think of it as "Internal Marketing".

But what is marketing?

I've discovered that the perception of what marketing's main function is fluctuates widely across industries, professions and social circles.

Have you ever met someone and think to yourself, "that guy looks like a Jeff..."? What caused you to feel that way?

Most likely there was a Jeff in your life with very distinct features or mannerisms that you subconsciously associate with that person. When you come across another person with these characteristics, your synapses fire and you think "That's a Jeff".

As humans, we "put things in boxes". We generalize and try to make associations among the things in our lives so that we can recall these more easily and more quickly. Stereotypes aren't always true, but often, they're pretty damn close!

So let's assume you've worked in an office for years where the marketing team's main function was making sure that there were flyers, pens and shirts available for the sales team to giveaway during a golf outing. Years later, you meet a person who works on another company's marketing team. Synapses fire, and "That's the pens and shirts guy".

Well... pens and shirts may be a fun strategy, but they don't have much to do with successfully bringing change to your slow and antiquated team.

Marketing is a multifaceted concept that involves promoting and selling products or services to customers. Marketers focus on understanding consumer needs and preferences in order to develop effective marketing campaigns. They conduct market research to analyze trends, identify potential markets, and gauge customer demand for specific products or services. By gathering data through surveys, interviews, and observations, marketers gain valuable insights into the wants of their target demographic.

So let's break down how Internal Marketing might work...

1. Begin with thorough research: Before proceeding with an internal marketing initiative, it is crucial to conduct comprehensive research in order to understand the needs and concerns of employees as well as potential barriers that may hinder their acceptance of change.

Has this been tried before? Who are the stakeholders? What is the current climate in the organization?

2.   Develop clear goals and objectives: Once you've done your research, clearly define the overall goals and objectives of the proposed changes alongside how they align with your company's vision. These should be communicated effectively using concise statements that leave no room for ambiguity.

Setting clear due dates. Being precise in what your expectations are of your teammates. Make sure your team knows what success looks like.

3. Craft persuasive messaging: To capture employee attention and drive interest toward the planned changes, craft persuasive messages tailored specifically to resonate with each department or team involved in the process.

Make sure you highlight the benefits, such as increased productivity or improved job satisfaction while addressing concerns proactively. "This will prevent you from having to do this dumb task every day."

4. Reach out through multiple channels: A successful marketing strategy employs diverse channels - not limiting communication to one medium alone but utilizing various formats like emails, newsletters, posters displayed across office spaces, intranet announcements or virtual town hall meetings - all catered towards different preferences of individuals within your company.

It often helps to put it in writing. People are busy. Create communication in mediums that can be revisited.

5. Offer training opportunities: Incorporate extensive training sessions into your internal marketing plan. Conduct workshops engaging experts who demonstrate skills required after implementation; empower employees and peers with practical exercises so they gain confidence regarding new processes.

Even better - record how you did it. Make that recording available and spread the word.

6. Provide regular updates: Keeping everyone up-to-date throughout an ongoing change process is vital. So offer regular progress reports via online platforms or interactive presentations. Allow questions to be addressed directly. Provide transparency regarding milestones achieved thus far, while also maintaining interest.

7. Encourage feedback and be responsive: Actively seeking employee feedback demonstrates respect for their opinions and concerns, and helps establish a culture of open communication. Provide platforms or mechanisms where individuals can voice their thoughts honestly and ensure prompt responses as this will keep them engaged.

As with any marketing strategy, it's going to take multiple touchpoints to drive adoption. By providing updates, you allow individuals the opportunity to revisit the idea after having time to acclimate.

8. Celebrate milestones & successes: While implementing change management and an internal marketing strategy un-doubtedly will involve some challenges, it is important to celebrate small wins along the journey to motivate employees further. Recognizing individual or team achievements fosters a positive environment encouraging everyone's commitment towards embracing future changes wholeheartedly.

Who are your early adopters? Leverage these folks as your advocates!

II

Where are we & how did we get here?

"It was easy to get in, but impossible to rise up."
Holly Flax

4

Aspiration

Being a motivated young professional is exhilarating. Every day is filled with a sense of purpose and drive. The constant desire to learn and grow fuels the fire within, propelling one forward on their chosen path. From setting ambitious goals to taking calculated risks, being motivated pervades every aspect of life. One cannot help but feel a surge of energy when tackling new challenges head-on.

The willingness to step outside of comfort zones becomes second nature, as one seeks personal and professional development relentlessly. It feels invigorating to push boundaries and continuously surpass previously set limitations. As a motivated young professional, the hunger for knowledge is insatiable. Meaningful experiences are sought out in order to gain valuable insights into various industries and fields of expertise. Books are devoured voraciously, providing both inspiration and guidance along this demanding journey toward success.

With motivation comes immense satisfaction from achieving

milestones - big or small. Each accomplishment signifies progress made towards dreams that were once mere figments of imagination; stepping stones leading towards an envisioned reality that now seems more tangible than ever before. There are moments when the weight of responsibility may feel over-whelming, but the unwavering motivation allows one to keep going despite adversity's presence. Difficulties encountered along the way serve merely as tests – opportunities for growth disguised as obstacles.

Motivated young professionals know no limits; they thrive on continuous improvement through honing existing skills while acquiring new ones with boundless enthusiasm. They embrace failure not as defeat but rather as valuable lessons learned paving the way toward better outcomes in future endeavors. At times it may be challenging to maintain that inner motivation amidst distractions or setbacks; however, true professionals persist regardless due to an unyielding belief in themselves and their abilities.

In essence, what it feels like to be a motivated young profes-sional can be described as a relentless pursuit of excellence guided by aspiration and determination fueling constant growth beyond expectations set by oneself or others around them.

As members of the Gen Z and Millennial generations begin their professional careers, it becomes crucial for them to make a significant impact at work. The importance of this lies in several key factors. Firstly, making an impact at work allows individuals to demonstrate their capabilities and talents. This generation faces fiercer competition than ever before due to advancements in technology and globalization. By showcasing their unique skills and abilities, young professionals can differentiate themselves from others, increasing their chances for career advancement and overall success.

Making an impact at work fosters personal fulfillment. Many individuals from these generations place great emphasis on finding meaning in their professional lives. They seek fulfilling work that aligns with their values and contributes positively to society or the greater good. Making a difference in the workplace offers a sense of purpose and satisfaction that enhances job satisfaction levels immensely.

Additionally, the desire to create change fuels innovation within organizations employing Gen Z and Millennial professionals. These newer generations possess fresh perspectives, adaptability, entrepreneurial spirit, as well as strong technological literacy – all qualities that facilitate unconventional thinking and problem-solving approaches. Companies benefit greatly when young professionals are encouraged to voice their ideas and actively contribute towards positive transformations.

Motivation is an inherent aspect of human nature, and the factors that drive young professionals at work are multifaceted and diverse. While monetary rewards are undeniably a key incentive for many individuals entering the workforce, it is vital to recognize that intrinsic motivators such as recognition, growth opportunities, and meaningful work play equally significant roles in fostering their enthusiasm. One of the most prevalent motivators for young professionals is the desire for recognition.

Aspiring and active young professionals yearn for validation from their peers and superiors alike; being acknowledged for their efforts significantly boosts self-esteem and morale. Whether through verbal praise or formal commendations during team meetings or company-wide events, this form of external affirmation acts as fuel to drive them toward continued success.

Young professionals seek continuous growth opportunities in their careers. They crave personal development through skill enhancement and acquiring new knowledge. Companies that offer training programs, mentorship initiatives or educational sponsorships establish an environment conducive to professional advancement—an environment where employees can thrive by constantly expanding their expertise within challenging fields they care deeply about.

Possessing a sense of purpose drives these individuals to excel in their professions. Young professionals aspire to engage with projects that align with their values and make a positive impact on society. The opportunity to contribute meaningfully inspires them both intrinsically—by fulfilling emotional needs—and extrinsically—with tangible evidence of making a difference— which further reinforces motivation levels at work.

Innovative corporations invest in creating supportive workplace cultures that foster collaboration among colleagues—a key driver for millennials specifically known for valuing teamwork highly. When others share ideas freely while encouraging creativity rather than competing solely against one another— individuals feel valued not just as contributors but also important members of cohesive groups working towards collective goals.

On another level entirely lies flexible work arrangements which provide much-needed autonomy enabling these motivated youngsters freedom over how they manage both professional responsibilities alongside personal obligations—an essential factor influencing job satisfaction positively among modern-day employees armed with technology that facilitates efficient remote work.

Young professionals are propelled by an intricate blend of factors which stem from both the extrinsic domains such as recognition and financial rewards to more innate drivers such as personal growth, meaningful work, collaborative environments, and workplace flexibility. By catering to these motivational cravings effectively throughout their careers, employers could help ensure optimal engagement among the next generation of talent aiming to make a lasting impact in the professional landscape.

However, few are the firms that have crafted such a grand playground for the young and restless professionals we're examining in this chapter.

5

De-Motivated

Once upon a time, in the bustling city of New York, there lived a young professional named Ethan. Fresh out of college with lofty ambitions and dreams that reached for the stars, he joined one of the most prestigious advertising agencies in town. Ethan possessed an unmatched drive and determination that had propelled him to excel at his work. He would stay late into the night brainstorming creative campaign ideas and relentlessly fine-tuning every detail until perfection was achieved. His colleagues admired his dedication to delivering excellence, and his superiors showered him with accolades.

In a bid to climb higher up the corporate ladder, Ethan pushed himself even harder each day. Days turned into weeks, weeks turned into months; he became consumed by nothing but his career aspirations. He lost count of countless moments spent away from friends and family, missing birthdays and anniversaries without giving it much thought. As time went on though, something began shifting within Ethan's restless soul. The relentless pursuit of success started sapping away pieces of his passion like leaves falling off an autumn tree.

One afternoon when gazing out over the city skyline from his office window—a sight that had once instilled hope in him—Ethan found no inspiration or motivation left within him anymore. Jogging on this treadmill towards success no longer held meaning for him; its rhythm had become monotonous. The spark in Ethan's eyes gradually faded as days blurred together through mundane presentations and meticulously crafted pitches devoid of genuine creativity. The joy he once found in seeing client satisfaction turned distant memories buried deep beneath layers of weariness. Soon enough, rumors whispered throughout the office about upcoming layoffs due to company-wide restructuring shook everyone's confidence; morale plummeted even further amongst employees already bearing witness to their own exhausted reflections through burnt candles.

Fear gnawed at Ethan like relentless waves crashing against rocks eroded over centuries—persistent yet unstoppable—and faith in himself waned under its weight. Nothing that emanated motivation, drive, or ambition remained within his hollowed-out core. Consequently, when the dreaded day arrived and Ethan found himself among those let go in a small box, he embraced the conclusion with resignation instead of desperation. A part of him mourned the loss of the dreams he once held with conviction—the passion and potential drowned amid countless restless nights at work. Months passed, but Ethan could no longer summon an ounce of interest to reignite his career flame. The fire that had blazed brightly became nothing more than ashes scattered by cruel winds across barren lands.

With each passing day in obscurity and mediocrity, grief consumed him as he pondered upon what might have been if only a choice was made differently—prioritizing human connections alongside professional goals.

Thus ends the story—an ode to one who sacrificed too much at the altar of ambition until left devoid of all life's simple joys—a lament for a young soul whose bright star fell from heavens untimely extinguished before time could caress its ethereal glow once more.

The light fades from our eyes...

There are several factors that can contribute to young professionals losing motivation. Firstly, the pressure to succeed in one's chosen career path can be overwhelming. When faced with high expectations and limited experience, it is common for individuals to feel as though they are constantly falling short. This constant sense of disappointment can lead to a lack of motivation and self-doubt.

Young professionals may become disillusioned by the reality of their chosen field. Often, idealistic visions of what a particular job or industry will entail don't align with the actual day-to-day responsibilities. This disconnect between expectation and reality can leave individuals feeling disheartened and unmotivated.

Workplace culture plays a significant role in an individual's level of motivation. Toxic environments characterized by long hours and little recognition can quickly sap one's enthusiasm for their work. Additionally, a lack of support or mentorship from colleagues or supervisors may hinder professional growth, causing individuals to lose faith in their abilities and subsequently lose motivation.

Burnout is increasingly prevalent among young professionals due to demanding workloads and an "always-on" mentality perpetuated by modern technology. The constant need to be connected and accessible not only affects work-life balance but also exhausts individuals mentally and emotionally over time. This exhaustion can easily lead these professionals to lose motivation as they struggle to find a sense of purpose amidst the relentless cycle of deadlines and commitments.

Personal circumstances outside of work can greatly impact one's level of motivation on the job. Financial stressors or family issues often take precedence over professional aspirations when young professionals find themselves juggling multiple responsibilities simultaneously.

Sadly but truly, there are various causes behind why young professionals may lose their drive at work—a combination of excessively high expectations undermining self-belief within inexperienced employees; unrealistic perceptions about careers clashing with real-world demands; toxic workplaces lacking encouragement; periods without adequate supervision suppressing progress possibilities while contributing generally lower support levels; rampant burnout resulting from constant connectivity demands with no separation from professional lives; and external personal pressures adding stress to the already-challenging work-life balance.

Recognizing these factors is crucial in addressing the issue and developing strategies that can help young professionals maintain their motivation, leading to overall career satisfaction and success.

6

Icons

Entrepreneurs, those who undertake the arduous journey of starting and running their businesses, have become a fascination to society.

The fame, attention, and glamour they receive from both their peers and larger society contribute to this mystique surrounding entrepreneurs. At first glance, it seems understandable why these individuals garner so much admiration. They embody success in the face of risk-taking and possess an unwavering determination that sets them apart.

However, a closer examination reveals that while there may be elements of truth behind the glorification of entrepreneurs, much of it is rooted in societal ideals rather than a comprehensive understanding of entrepreneurship itself.

One reason for the elevated status enjoyed by entrepreneurs is the allure associated with financial success. Financial achievements are universally recognized as markers of prestige in today's capitalistic world. Entrepreneurs often generate wealth through their businesses; thus, economic prosperity becomes emblematic of their entrepreneurial prowess. Their ability to amass fortunes seemingly overnight instills envy among many who aspire to follow suit or wish they had taken similar risks earlier in life.

Popular culture plays an excessive role in perpetuating this image thanks to shows like "Shark Tank" or movies like "The Social Network," where stories showcase staggering commercial successes against all odds. These media portrayals present a highly romanticized version of entrepreneurship; however fictionalized or selective they may be based on real-life stories! Consequently, whether intentionally or not derivated tales leave audiences desiring such financial triumphs without comprehending fully the various struggles entailed in the initial stages.

Society's obsession with glamorizing entrepreneurs can be attributed to the rise of the gig economy and its eccentric marvels.

The gig economy, characterized by short-term contracts or freelance work, has given birth to a new breed of self-employed individuals who embody the spirit of entrepreneurship. This newfound admiration for those daring enough to deviate from traditional employment models has led society to place these entrepreneurs on a pedestal.

One reason behind this glorification is the perception that entrepreneurs possess an extraordinary level of autonomy and freedom in their careers. Unlike conventional workers bound by rigid schedules and hierarchical structures, entrepreneurs appear unhampered by such constraints. They are seen as masters of their own destinies - navigating through professional challenges at their own pace, charting unconventional career paths while pursuing personal passions.

Social media, aside from its unfounded level-setting ability in the business world, plays a pivotal role in perpetuating this fascination with entrepreneurs. Platforms like Instagram have become fertile ground for showcasing impressive lifestyles, exotic locations, luxurious homes and cars associated with entrepreneurial success. Scrolling through carefully curated feeds filled with images that scream opulence and prosperity reinforces society's view that entrepreneurship equates to living a magical life where dreams manifest effortlessly.

It is absolutely crucial to question whether this infatuation truly captures the reality faced by most entrepreneurs operating within the gig economy framework. Beyond the filter-less glamour lies countless stories of struggle emanating from individuals taking uncertain steps along uncharted paths laden with risks and uncertainty.

Despite societal expectations tied to becoming an entrepreneur amid today's gig economy craze, there are profound challenges considerably different from those encountered within traditional business ventures or steady jobs supported by well-established firms. Entrepreneurs functioning within gig economies frequently experience unstable income streams due to unpredictable project cycles requiring relentless hustle towards new ventures time after time without stability usually afforded by regular 9-to-5 positions corporations commonly provide for.

Contrary to the popular belief that entrepreneurs have complete control - the fulfillment of contracts and deliverables without any guarantees, truly encapsulates the chaotic reality. These self-employed individuals are burdened with strenuous demands; they shoulder legal, accounting wedded on top core vocational obligations sometimes complicating otherwise radiant lifestyles with significant facets overlooked when glorified.

It's imperative for society to acknowledge the perplexing truths reflective of most entrepreneurial efforts intertwined within gig-economy eccentric marvels rather than focusing solely on outward facades or overstated luxuries. By appreciating the difficulties faced by these pioneers genuinely, we can nurture a more realistic understanding of entrepreneurship and strive towards cultivating an environment where innovators feel supported through numerous challenges encountered along their journeys.

7

Corporate Drones

I think we've all heard the phrase, "I feel like just a number at work". This may be in part due to a phenomenon known as the *educational-industrial complex.*

This education complex is humanity's way of industrially creating worker bees for this economic machine we call the World. The question is, *why?*

To answer that, we have to go back to the roots of our modern educational system. Back to the Industrial Revolution. Back to the time when factories were sprouting up everywhere, and they needed workers, obedient workers, and largely, workers who could follow instructions. Hello there, schools, the perfect breeding grounds for just that. Out of those educational institutions, were churned out literate and numerate individuals who could read, write, calculate, and follow orders without questioning authority.

Imagine if you will, a school is not a school at all, but a factory.

And its raw material is not metal or plastic, but children. And its final product is a perfect adult worker who fits nice and snug into the little factory so carefully labeled Society. And the final assembly line that assembles these nice and neat rows of adult workers, consists of a standardized curriculum, standardized tests, and a standardized grading system. It's an assembly line of education, with zero room left for creativity, innovation, or individuality.

But the era of the Industrial Age has come, and gone. What keeps standing in its way like a stubborn old man, is the Industrial Age education. And the question is, *if we don't live in the Industrial Age anymore, then why are we still using our Industrial Age educating methods?*

And I think the answer is simple. **It is because it is easy.** It is much easier to measure progress with standardized tests, and to rank students and cut the threshold off at a grade, than it is to measure creativity or critical thinking. It is much easier to assume that that great big lump in the cranium is just stored with *knowledge* than it is to nourish individuality or dreams.

Let me lay a small scenario in your mind. Imagine a classroom. A room where children are taught not what they need to think, nor in what particular organized textbook method they should think, but encouraged to think for themselves. What does that sound like to you? Chaotic? Messy? Chaotic and messy consequences that nobody wants to face? Because there's no formula on the paper to apply and write down and just turn in.

This is going to be dirty. It's going to be unpredictable. It's going to be unorganized. But it's also where the magic happens. The learning happens. That is where we try not to set foot. We started with the notion of creating thinkers, but the education system finds the task too daunting. So, to be consistent with our failure, we only create worker bees.

Now, I'm guessing you're thinking worker bees are a good thing? Yes, yes they most certainly are. Sometimes we even yearn for just the perfect little beehive. When bees are happy. When they are engaged with the nectar they're collecting, nurturing the larvae, and protecting the hive from its enemies.

We're okay with that.

The difference between a beehive and the society we live in is that in a beehive, not every bee can be a queen bee. Not every worker bee has the potential to be a queen bee. But in our society, every single individual has the potential to be a queen bee. The potential to be the innovator, the leader, to be the visionary.

Yet the educational complex, with its efficiency and control, is snuffing that right out. It's like we're stuck in a never-ending game of Whac-A-Mole, where we're just training moles to pop up and down on cue, rather than producing innovative thinkers. The arcade needs a new game.

> *Instead of wondering when your next vacation is, maybe you should set up a life you don't need to escape from. – Seth Godin*

We should create an education system that passionate students will never wish to escape. An education system that advocates curiosity, inquiry, and self; over uniformity, and blind memorization; An education system that will serve as a bridge, from where we are today, to the future we hope to be one day.

And if you really think about it, the question isn't whether we should have worker bees?

The question is, *can we afford to only have worker bees?*

Think of it.

In fact, the hive always needs workers, but the hive also always needs the queen bee as well. The queen bee, who lays the eggs, who ensures that the colony will survive to see another day.

For decades, schools have been seen as a system for producing factory workers. From an early age, we learn that success comes from following instructions, memorizing information, and fitting tidily into tidy little rows. The focus is particularly acute in STEM, where even the most informal engineering education systems pass on information about how to hold the soldering iron, what order to load a static compiler, and how to solo up a sequencer.

However, entrepreneurship, far from being a way to get a B– in Constructive Conformity, is about seeing (and working on) problems that others don't; it may be one of the last ways to function in our individual futures (just ask any journalist). It is literally a set of methods for identifying problems to solve. And that's what makes someone who is self-directed; driven to build and distribute their own independent projects.

Let's take a look at the work of Matt Heiman.

Matt Heiman is a luminary - eminent and original - in the field of business strategy and entrepreneurship. His mission is to light the way for established companies to become able to do what successful entrepreneurial ventures do. And his strategy is to help them get there in a fashion that is anything but a one-size-fits-all approach.

Here's what he does. He starts his work by doing a hard-headed assessment of a company's existing operational underpinnings to see which of them — typically the ones that date back many decades — robs the firm of the ability to engage with new developments in business and technology.

He then goes to work to put whatever parts of the company insist on maintaining practices that are anachronistic in the areas of creativity, risk-taking, and problem-solving into a different light. That's entrepreneurial light, of course. That's the only kind of light that works to create the sort of environment that enables start-up companies to thrive - all while working to give the broader company a nimble, agile mindset so that it can keep up in a fast and ever-changing marketplace. Just like a new business would. That's a company in which all parts of the organization demonstrated a fierce ability to keep learning and adapting and to keep going even in moments of uncertainty.

And on top of all that, he also works to find distinct but potentially transformative opportunities in the market for the company. Then he helps the company take advantage of them, breaking ground in exactly the way that new firms try to do. This turns a company not only into one that can survive in its industry.

For example - let's look at his work at TechRevolution.

Heiman began by conducting a comprehensive assessment of the company's operations, which surfaced two issues: First, TechRevolution's technology infrastructure was outdated, and second, the firm lacked an adequate project management system.

To begin, the outmoded systems in place were sapping resources and limiting TechRevolution's ability to grow. His solution: Migrate TechRevolution to a cloud-based system. In moving to the cloud, the company was able to automate many mundane activities — most notably, the handling of HR paperwork — and also was able to reduce the cost of absorbing new business.

Once TechRevolution's back end had been modernized, Heiman designed Agile project management processes to replace older ways of working.

Quick Explanation...

The traditional "Plan, Do, Stop, Correct" (PDSC) model involves a structured and linear approach to project management. In this model, a detailed plan is formulated at the start of the project, followed by the execution phase. The process then stops to allow for assessment and correction of errors. This approach entails a higher risk of late error detection and does not adapt quickly to changes.

On the other hand, Agile's "Analyze, Design, Code, Test" (ADCT) model promotes an iterative and incremental process. Each cycle or 'sprint' involves analysis, designing, coding, and testing of a portion of the whole project. This allows for quick error detection and correction, and it's highly adaptable to changes, which makes it suitable for projects with uncertain or volatile requirements. However, the Agile model requires a high level of customer and team involvement throughout the development process.

In summary, the way Heimann showed TechRevolution how they could break work into pieces meant that the company's employees, quickly, could see the progress they were making, and that ensured that they didn't drift away from the core mission.

III

#GOALS

"Everyone thinks of changing the world, but no one
thinks of changing himself."
Leo Tolstoy

8

The Stretch Goal

Setting stretch goals at work can be a highly effective way to push yourself beyond your limits and achieve outstanding results. By challenging the status quo and striving for ambitious objectives, you not only enhance your professional growth but also contribute to the overall success of your team and organization. To successfully set stretch goals, it is important to follow a systematic approach that involves clear communication, proper planning, regular tracking of progress, and continuous adaptation.

The first step in setting stretch goals is to clearly communicate with stakeholders about what exactly constitutes as a stretch goal. Ambiguity should be avoided here because without a precise understanding of expectations, both personal and organizational alignment may suffer. For instance, if you aim for 20% increase in sales within three months rather than vague statements like "improving sales," everyone involved will have an explicit target to strive towards.

Once clarity has been established around the desired outcomes, the next step is careful planning to determine how these targets can be achieved. This entails breaking down the larger goal into smaller manageable tasks or milestones that need to be accomplished along the way.

As you start working towards your stretch goals, it is crucial to regularly track your progress. This not only keeps you accountable but also allows you to make necessary adjustments along the way. By monitoring key performance indicators along with evaluating potential roadblocks or setbacks encountered during your journey, you can ensure timely corrective actions and stay on course toward achieving your desired outcomes.

Continuously adapt as needed to face challenges effectively in pursuit of stretch goals. Flexibility and resilience are essential qualities for success when setting ambitious targets because circumstances may evolve or unforeseen obstacles may arise that require alternative approaches or modifications to initially planned strategies. Being open-minded, seeking feedback from mentors or colleagues, learning from mistakes, and making necessary improvements will enable continuous growth throughout the process.

SMART Goals

The idea of SMART goals was originally invented by George T. Doran back in 1981. With the increasing need for professionals to effectively set and achieve their objectives, he recognized the importance of a framework that could guide individuals toward success. SMART is an acronym that stands for Specific, Measurable, Achievable, Relevant and Time-bound - each element serving a unique purpose in goal-setting.

SMART goals ensure clarity and focus. By clearly defining what needs to be accomplished, professionals are able to direct their efforts appropriately and avoid any confusion or ambiguity surrounding their objectives. This eliminates room for mis-interpretation and enables individuals to have a clear vision of what they aim to achieve.

Incorporating measurability into goal setting allows profession-als to establish criteria against which progress can be tracked effectively. By establishing precise metrics or targets related to their goals, individuals can easily evaluate whether they are moving closer toward accomplishing them or if adjustments need to be made along the way. In this manner, failure becomes an opportunity for reevaluation rather than simply an obstacle.

Ensuring that goals remain achievable contributes significantly towards maintaining motivation levels among professionals who passionately strive for innovation. Often faced with com-plex challenges which demand creativity and resourcefulness on multiple fronts simultaneously these opportunities can feel overwhelming without proper guidance.

Therefore, defining specific milestones within realistic bound-aries helps create shorter-term victories alongside the ultimate objective which reignites motivation during long challenging periods. Another important aspect addressed by SMART goals is relevance-oriented planning. The "R" prompts professionals working towards innovation-related objectives to assess how aligned their ambitions are with both organizational priorities as well as personal aspirations. By doing so it enhances strategic positioning & minimizes conflicts between individual professional values vs. larger organization missions aligning energy in commendable manners leading to optimal results.

The emphasis placed on time-bound task management pushes forward momentum throughout project lifecycles. Deadlines bring about a sense of accountability in professionals knowing their performance will be objectively evaluated creating a sense of urgency, refining resource allocation & reinforcing commitment-based prioritizing.

Therefore, completing tasks on schedule ensures that long-term goals are not lost amidst the flurry of daily activities and fosters consistency in professional innovation. In conclusion, SMART goals were developed to assist professionals in achieving success through clearly defined and manageable objectives. The specificity, measurability, achievability, relevance, and time-bound nature of these goals provide professionals with a structured approach that facilitates effective planning and progress assessment.

By incorporating these elements into their goal-setting process, individuals are able to maximize productivity, maintain motivation, strategically position themselves within organizations as well as personal ambitions, and ensure constant innovation.

9

Fire Drills

Once upon a time, in a bustling city, there lived an office worker named Sarah. Sarah was known for her never-ending schedule and perpetually chaotic workspace. From the moment she stepped foot in the office until long after everyone had gone home, she would dart from one task to another with unyielding determination.

On any given day, Sarah's desk resembled a tornado-ravaged disaster zone - papers strewn haphazardly, sticky notes clinging desperately to edges of her computer monitor like colorful vines. Her coworkers often marveled at how she managed to function amidst such disarray. Meetings were a constant presence on Sarah's jam-packed agenda; every minute of her workday accounted for by appointments that seemed to multiply like rabbits.

As soon as one meeting concluded, she dashed off urgently to join the next without even sparing a thought about organizing herself in between. Her colleagues admired (and secretly envied) her tenacity but lamented their inability to decipher or predict what madness lay beneath all those hoops through which Sarah effortlessly leapt. She was constantly juggling multiple projects in various stages of completion, never slowing down enough to contemplate if quality might be sacrificed for quantity.

As Murphy's Law dictated when it comes to busy individuals such as Sarah: chaos attracts chaos. Emails poured into her inbox faster than raindrops during monsoon season – urgent requests buried amidst reply-all threads that multiplied endlessly – each demanding immediate attention and action surpassing human capability.

Sarah clung tightly onto sanity by merely relying on mental notes rather than relying on tangible reminders; undoubtedly an impressive feat but not without its inevitable consequences. Shouts of "did you send me that report yet?" frequented this exact question mark hanging over anyone who dared cross paths with our perplexingly efficient protagonist.

The insidious whispers around the water cooler questioned whether someone so dedicated could really continue successfully living life untamed amidst exuberant bedlam? But alas! While the walls of Sarah's cubicle may tell a tale that would raise eyebrows even among tornado-chasers, there was a method to her madness.

One fateful day, as luck would have it, someone equipped with organizational prowess entered Sarah's life. This mysterious individual presented her with an elegant planner - meticulously designed to meet dizzying deadlines and multitasking miracles.

With newfound tools at her disposal, Sarah hesitated before embracing this foreign notion of structure but decided against ignoring a turning point delivering solace from perpetual disarray. As colors splashed across calendar blocks detailing actual timelines for tasks rather than fearfully worded scribbles hastily scratched on sticky notes.

Gradually, order returned like long-lost pieces meticulously aligning into place in some grand puzzle she had constructed years ago whilst drowning in the labyrinthine chaos Sara once called home. And so it came to pass; deadlines were met consistently while permitting breathing room within those crammed schedules – coworkers' raised eyebrows transformed into awe-struck applause for her splendid metamorphosis.

Nothing is a fire when everything is a fire.

"Chris, how's it going?"

"Oh, just putting out fires..."

It seems that nothing is urgent when everything is urgent. The constant influx of tasks, responsibilities, and deadlines often leaves us feeling overwhelmed and unable to prioritize effectively. When everything becomes urgent, our ability to assign importance to each task diminishes. As a result, we find ourselves trying desperately to tackle every demand simultaneously.

When faced with an endless list of urgencies, it appears that our perception of urgency itself becomes distorted. Our minds become accustomed to the perpetual state of urgency in which we are constantly operating. Consequently, even the most pressing matters fail to ignite the same sense of urgency within us as they should.

This pervasive culture of urgency stemming from multiple sources can lead to detrimental effects on our well-being. Experiencing chronic stress and anxiety due to various demands takes a toll on both our physical and mental health. We may struggle with sleeplessness or fatigue brought about by consistently working under intense pressure.

When everything is considered equally important or time-sensitive, decision-making becomes arduous and inefficient. Without clear priorities or distinctions between what requires immediate attention and what can wait patiently in line behind other tasks allows important matters slip through the cracks.

Striking a balance amidst all these perceived urgencies becomes paramount for ensuring productivity while maintaining personal well-being. It is crucial that we equip ourselves with effective tools for managing overwhelming situations such as creating comprehensive schedules or practicing mindfulness techniques that allow us clarity amid chaos.

We have to recognize that not everything can be truly urgent at once – there will always be varying degrees of priority among different obligations. By reframing how we approach urgency and prioritization – understanding its relativity rather than accepting every task as equally critical – we regain control over our hectic lives and pave the way towards more meaningful achievements without compromising our inner peace.

10

Change

Once upon a time, in a bustling town filled with ambitious entrepreneurs and thriving businesses, there was a company called Exemplar Corp. Known for its cutting-edge technology and innovative ideas back in the day, it had once occupied the top spot in the industry. However, as time passed by and technology evolved at an exponential rate, Exemplar Corp became increasingly resistant to change.

At first glance, everything seemed perfectly fine within the walls of this once-prominent company. The employees diligently carried out their tasks without questioning outdated processes or exploring new possibilities. Management held firmly onto traditional strategies while disregarding emerging trends happening right before their eyes.

As years went by, competitors rose to prominence by embracing novel approaches and adapting quickly to market demands. Their flexibility allowed them to stay ahead of the curve while offering enhanced products and services that customers craved.

Even though murmurs of caution circulated internally about being left behind amidst these changes, Exemplar Corp remained stubbornly rooted in old-fashioned practices.

The decline of this fictional corporation was slow but steady—a slippery slope initiated solely by their resistance to change. Gradually they lost touch with market dynamics; profit margins dwindled year after year as innovative companies flourished around them; talented employees began seeking employment elsewhere where growth opportunities were abundant.

Throughout these insipid times for the business world legends materialized about how stagnant air enveloped every corner of Exemplar's office space – furtive glances exchanged between frustrated team members struggling under outdated systems; an esprit de corps slowly replaced by apathy towards progress; brainstorming sessions visibly lacking inspiration or enthusiasm.

Customers also took notice of this gradual decay within the formerly exalted organization: loyal clients who had been passionate advocates for years now turned away due to jaded interactions with customer service representatives unable—or unwilling—to address evolving needs.

Finally coming face-to-face with imminent failure sinking deep in their bones awakened some urgency within upper management ranks. Management aimed to breathe life back into their crumbling empire by implementing a massive internal overhaul project called "Revitalize." However, it was too little, too late.

The change agents brought in were skilled at their craft but struggled against the firm resistance still present within some employees' hearts. Rebuilding trust and enthusiasm proved to be an arduous task amidst years of skepticism and disillusionment.

Ultimately, Exemplar Corp closed its doors as whispers of missed opportunities lingered throughout the industry. The fictional company found itself etched into entrepreneurial folklore—a tale warning others about the dire consequences of being resistant to change; a cautionary story teaching us to embrace innovation instead of succumbing to stagnation; a vision illustrating how organizations failing adaptability face gradual decline until they become mere relics in their own history books.

And thus ended the saga of Exemplar Corp—an unpredictable turn for an enterprise that once stood tall but refused evolution when it mattered most.

Change Management

Change management is an essential process utilized successfully in corporations for enhancing organizational performance and adapting to evolving business environments effectively. Through the implementation of change management strategies and techniques, companies aim to navigate transitions smoothly, minimize resistance from employees, and ensure sustainable growth.

One way change management is leveraged effectively at corporations is by creating a clear vision for the proposed changes. By establishing a well-defined goal or direction, organizations can provide their employees with a sense of purpose and understanding about why the changes are necessary. With this clarity, individuals can align their efforts with the overall objectives, promoting unity and cooperation within the corporate ecosystem.

Successful change management involves effective communication throughout every phase of transformation. The dissemination of timely information regarding upcoming changes helps alleviate anxiety or uncertainty among employees. Clear communication channels facilitate transparency while allowing staff members to voice concerns or ask questions about modifications taking place. This exchange fosters trust between management and workers as they feel included in decision-making processes rather than passively observing from the sidelines.

Incorporating stakeholder engagement into a change management strategy ensures better utilization of available expertise while fostering ownership over proposed transformations within corporations. Consulting key stakeholders affected by changes enables organizations to gain diverse perspectives that may contribute valuable insights or suggestions during the planning stages. Furthermore, involving different levels of staff in the decision-making process creates a collective responsibility toward achieving desired outcomes more efficiently.

Another significant aspect leading to successful change deployment lies in providing ample training opportunities for employees affected by new processes or technologies being introduced into the corporation's operations. Training programs empower staff members with the necessary skills while equipping them with the confidence needed when navigating these unfamiliar territories during transitional periods.

Implementing feedback loops allows continuous learning from experiences encountered during each stage of transition - be it successes or obstacles faced along the way—thus enabling rapid adjustments when deemed essential based on emerging insights accumulated through regular feedback mechanisms implemented within corporations that support sustainable transformational outcomes.

Successful change management also necessitates recognizing and addressing potential resistance from employees during periods of transition. Change often disrupts established routines and can create uncertainty or fear among staff members, leading to reluctance in embracing modifications. It is **vital** for corporations to identify the sources of resistance related to change and implement suitable strategies, such as communication initiatives or employee involvement programs, aimed at mitigating concerns and promoting acceptance.

Monitoring change management efforts can contribute toward its success. By tracking progress against predetermined metrics throughout the process, organizations can identify areas that require course correction while also celebrating milestones achieved along the way. Regularly assessing the impact of changes ensures that they align with desired outcomes while allowing subsequent modifications if required.

11

Calculated Risks

Developing an intrapreneur mindset requires several strategies, and two of the most important ones are taking calculated risks and embracing change. By adopting these approaches, individuals can cultivate a mindset that encourages innovation and drive within established organizations.

One effective strategy for developing an intrapreneur mindset is the art of taking calculated risks. Rather than blindly stepping into unknown territories, those seeking to foster an intrapreneurial spirit analyze the potential rewards and consequences associated with a particular endeavor. It involves careful evaluation, thorough research, and realistic goal-setting. By weighing the pros and cons, intrapreneurs can determine whether a risk is worth taking. They understand that failure does not signify incompetence but serves as a valuable learning opportunity.

In addition to taking calculated risks, embracing change is another crucial strategy in fostering an intrapreneurial mindset.

In today's fast-paced world, businesses must continually adapt to remain competitive. Intrapreneurs recognize this reality and proactively embrace change as a catalyst for growth rather than viewing it merely as a disruption. Instead of resisting new ideas or methods within an organization, they actively seek ways to drive innovation and advocate for necessary adjustments in order to stay ahead of the curve.

Along with prudent risk-taking comes another essential approach to building an intrapreneurial mindset – your readiness to welcome change with open arms.

Embracing change paves the way for success, as individuals who actively welcome new experiences open themselves up to a plethora of opportunities. Possessing a readiness to adapt and adjust their mindset fosters personal growth and allows for creative solutions to arise. Rather than shy away from uncertainty, those who welcome change with open arms demonstrate flexibility, resilience, and the ability to thrive in unpredictable situations.

By actively seeking change and novel experiences, individuals challenge themselves to step outside of their comfort zones. This willingness to confront uncomfortable situations expands one's horizons and broadens their perspectives. Success no longer becomes limited by reservation but grows boundlessly through the exploration of the unknown.

Embracing change demonstrates one's adaptability in both personal and professional environments. In today's rapidly evolving world, the rate of technological advancements calls for individuals who can quickly learn new skills or reinvent themselves when necessary. When faced with changes in job requirements or technologies, those who are ready to embrace unfamiliar territory often emerge victorious.

Welcoming change manifests as an essential quality for effective leadership. Successful leaders understand that progress relies on innovation; they recognize that holding onto old practices inhibits growth. By advocating for changes within organizational strategies or models of operation, leaders encourage innovation while shaping a dynamic work environment.

In addition to fostering personal growth and adapting effectively in various scenarios, embracing change provides an avenue for creative problem solving - critical components of success both professionally and personally. The ability to adjust one's perspective opens doors previously unseen; it challenges preconceived notions and engenders unique solutions that would have been left undiscovered by those resistant to change.

Nevertheless, preparing oneself mentally contributes greatly toward embracing change successfully. It requires developing a positive mindset that perceives transitions as opportunities rather than obstacles — perceiving change as advantageous propels one towards success while inspiring others along the way.

Enabling calculated risk-taking while also storing optimism & enthusiasm towards inevitable organizational changes can pave the way for building an incisive intrapreneurial insight.

Embracing a positive outlook and fostering genuine enthusiasm toward organizational changes can have profound effects on your individual growth. By storing such optimistic energy, individuals are more likely to become intrapreneurs, harnessing their resourcefulness and creativity to navigate the evolving landscape. This mindset shift contributed by an intrapreneurial acuity can pave the way for innovative solutions, efficient processes, and an overall increased productivity within an organization.

Foremost, storing optimistic enthusiasm creates a foundation for open-mindedness. When you are genuinely excited about upcoming changes, you will become amazed how you begin to approach them with curiosity rather than resistance. This receptiveness allows you to explore new opportunities presented by organizational shifts.

Additionally, this positive mindset leads to greater adaptability in the face of change. Enthusiastic individuals tend to embrace discomfort as an opportunity for learning and improvement rather than viewing it as a hindrance or threat to their current status quo. They develop resilience and quickly adjust strategies or approaches when necessary – crucial qualities for success in today's fast-paced business environment.

Optimism provides a strong catalyst for cultivating an intrapreneurial spirit within organizations. Intrapreneurs possess attributes like initiative, proactiveness, and resourcefulness that drive progress during uncertain times.

Developing an intrapreneur mindset demands careful consideration of tactics like taking calculated risks and embracing change. To achieve growth and foster innovation within established organizations, individuals must become adept at analyzing risks intelligently, welcoming change as a driver of progress rather than resisting it. Employing these strategies, coupled with a few of the ideas explored above, is a surefire way toward an inspiring intrapreneurial journey.

IV

A New Hope

"Hope is like the sun. If you only believe in it when you can see it, you'll never make it through the night."
Leia Organa

12

Indago

*This is where we start examining specific examples of intrapreneurs worth studying (repeatedly!). They figured out a plan for what the hell you **can** do. They were determined to figure out how you **can** make a difference. They may not have invented the light bulb, but they did get their team to accomplish some amazing things.*

My first exposure to the concept of intrapreneurship found me in the back row of seats on the 51-Outbound bus. Doom scrolling through social media and "I'm honored and humbled to accept a position in a bullcrap firm, which I got because I went to the right school and never really had a hard life" LinkedIn posts... I stumbled upon the story of Lockheed Martin and their advancement of the idea of intrapreneurship.

Lockheed Martin's journey into intrapreneurship began in the late 1990s when they introduced their Skunk Works program. This initiative aimed to create a small team of passionate individuals who would operate independently from bureaucratic procedures and embrace an entrepreneurial mindset. Skunk

Works became renowned for generating groundbreaking ideas and fostering an environment where innovation thrived.

One notable example of intrapreneurial success at Lockheed Martin is seen through Indago, an unmanned aerial vehicle (UAV) system developed internally by their skunk works team. The project was initiated by several engineers who recognized the potential market for UAV technology long before it gained widespread popularity. With limited resources but abundant determination, these intrapreneurs leveraged their expertise to develop a lightweight UAV capable of versatile surveillance missions. Their breakthrough came with designing unique foldable wings that allowed ease of transportation while maintaining endurance in-flight capability.

The Indago prototype quickly caught the attention of Lockheed Martin's executive leadership due to its impressive capabilities and promising market prospects. Recognizing its tremendous commercial value as well as military applications such as reconnaissance and disaster response missions, Lockheed Martin invested further resources into refining this revolutionary technology. Through effective collaboration between the skunk works team members and other divisions within Lockheed Martin, Indago evolved from a mere concept to a fully realized product ready for deployment.

In addition to government contracts securing steady revenue streams, the company expanded its customer base significantly by catering to various industries' specific needs like agriculture monitoring or infrastructure inspection with adaptations tailored accordingly. This triumph serves as evidence that embracing intrapreneurship has propelled Lockheed Martin towards novel opportunities while elevating industry standards through continuous technological advancements.

Indago's success exemplifies the potential for large corporations to embrace intrapreneurial spirit by providing employees with autonomy, resources, and incentives necessary for new ideas to flourish. In conclusion, Lockheed Martin's adoption of intrapreneurship through initiatives like Skunk Works has paved the way for successful projects such as Indago. By utilizing entrepreneurial principles within their corporate environment, Lockheed Martin encourages a culture of creativity and risk-taking that leads to innovation in various sectors. This transformative journey showcases how intrapreneurship can drive growth and establish industry leaders amidst an ever-changing business landscape.

13

Fry

Innovation and creativity, regarded as key drivers of success for any organization, often face challenges when brought to established companies due to bureaucratic structures and resistance to change. However, Art Fry, the inventor of the iconic Post-it Note, managed to overcome these obstacles by navigating the internal culture of 3M, making him a remarkable intrapreneur.

Crucial to Fry's success was his ability to understand and leverage the existing culture at 3M. Being a renowned multinational conglomerate known for its commitment to innovation and giving employees the freedom to explore their ideas played a significant role in his achievements. Recognizing this culture proved fruitful for Fry.

The unique philosophy at 3M is evident in its "15% Time" policy—a practice that allows employees to spend fifteen percent of their time on personal projects—encouraging exploration and risk-taking. Acknowledging the significance of this autonomy-driven culture propelled Fry towards developing his revolutionary invention. Driven by his passion for organizing and problem-solving everyday issues, Fry invented the universally known Post-it Note after recognizing his need for an adhesive bookmark that would stick without damaging church hymnals.

Teaming up with Spencer Silver—who had developed a low-tack adhesive—the pair experimented tirelessly until they produced a product that adhered perfectly while being re-stickable without leaving residue. Despite facing skepticism within the company about the potential impact of his creation, including initial resistance from colleagues who failed to initially grasp its value; Fry pressed forward thanks again to understanding what makes 3M's workplace tick; persisting in pushing development efforts further despite hurdles persisted internally.

Collaboration played an equally crucial part in Fry's journey as an intrapreneur within 3M: recognizing it highlighted opportunities beyond generating expertise insight into enhancing products effectively aiding support measures dedicated toward reaping benefits resulting in cultivating teamwork essential towards sharing responsibilities driving success even further defining milestones like successful promotion strategies extended way one-directionally by receiving benefits interaction driving growth mutually beneficial and coherent to every party within the company they work in.

Persistence acted as a pivotal attribute in Fry's accomplishments too. No matter what challenges he encountered, setbacks didn't deter him; instead, they served as a fire, stoking the engine and reevaluating strategy, refining products, which further demonstrated his versatility.

Art Fry's remarkable story bears testimony to the power of creating an environment conducive for intrapreneurship within an organization - his understanding and incorporation of 3M's culture synonymous with their empowered employees generated a novelty outcome.

14

Jobs

Steve Jobs, the legendary co-founder of Apple Inc., is widely praised for his visionary leadership and revolutionary contributions to the technology industry. Nonetheless, it is essential to acknowledge that behind these accomplishments lies an often-neglected attribute: his profound intrapreneurial spirit.

Possessing an innate drive and relentless ambition, Jobs embarked on a journey that not only reshaped Apple but also paved the way for innovative advancements across the entire tech landscape. Intrapreneurship can be defined as acting like an entrepreneur within a pre-existing organization. By seizing this opportunity within Apple, Jobs demonstrated unparalleled initiative which propelled him towards groundbreaking achievements.

His ability to think outside conventional boundaries enabled him to challenge established norms and completely transform how technology was perceived and experienced by consumers worldwide. Throughout his career at Apple, Steve Jobs spearheaded numerous ambitious projects that defied industry standards. From envisioning sleek personal computers such as the Macintosh in 1984 to launching game-changing devices like the iPod in 2001 and unveiling cutting-edge smartphones like the iPhone in 2007, Jobs harnessed his entrepreneurial instincts with remarkable success while operating within a corporate setting.

What set Jobs apart from others was not just his undeniable creativity, but also his unwavering determination in pursuing perfection; a trait often associated with successful entrepreneurs. Sure, every product released under Jobs' stewardship embodied innovation tempered by exacting attention to detail—an unrivaled combination that resonated deeply with consumers - consequently cementing Apple's position as one of the most influential companies in history.

Beyond mere technological devices, Steve Jobs also focused on harmonizing bold design aesthetics with intuitive user interfaces—a testament to his unmatched penchant for seamless integration between hardware and software elements. Pioneering this approach gave rise to a paradigm shift where users could interact effortlessly with novel technologies embodied within beautifully crafted devices – ultimately revolutionizing consumer expectations throughout the digital age.

The impact of Steve Job's intrapreneurial ingenuity reached beyond Apple, establishing a transformative ripple effect throughout the tech industry at large. His relentless pursuit of excellence and his constant reimagining of what was deemed possible opened new horizons for countless individuals who sought to push boundaries and emulate Jobs' daring within their respective companies.

While Steve Jobs is rightfully celebrated as a visionary leader who revolutionized the tech industry with innovation, this recognition must extend to acknowledging his remarkable intrapreneurial spirit. By embodying traits typically associated with entrepreneurs,a persistent drive, and an uncanny ability to challenge conventions, Jobs propelled Apple's meteoric rise and fundamentally reshaped our relationship with technology. Impacting both Apple and the wider tech landscape.Jobs left behind a formidable legacy that will continue to inspire generations of innovators seeking to follow in his footsteps.

15

Godin

Godin's success as an intrapreneur can be attributed to his skill in establishing and nurturing relationships. At Spinnaker Software, Godin was able to foster connections with colleagues in various departments by taking the initiative to communicate and collaborate effectively. This enabled him to gain insights from different perspectives and contributed to the successful implementation of his innovative ideas.

During his time at Seth Godin Productions, Godin proved himself as a reliable partner by building trusting relationships with clients and collaborators. By actively listening and demonstrating genuine interest in their needs, he was able to create customized marketing strategies that significantly improved client satisfaction and loyalty.

While working at Yahoo, Godin showcased exceptional relationship-building skills by forming strong alliances with individuals across hierarchies. His ability to connect with professionals at all levels allowed him not only to understand diverse viewpoints but also garner support for his initiatives. Through these relationships, Godin positioned himself as a knowledgeable resource who could provide valuable insights related specifically to marketing.

The significance of building strong professional relationships extends beyond individual achievements; it creates a work environment conducive for collaboration and growth. Strong connections enable effective communication within teams, increasing productivity and fostering innovation through the exchange of ideas from diverse perspectives.

When employees have established solid rapport among themselves or with clients/customers/vendors/ partners/suppliers (whichever it is) they are more likely to feel supported, which increases morale within the organization, resulting in positive overall job satisfaction levels and aiding retention rates reducing employee turnover.

Building lasting connections also enhances trust between colleagues enabling smoother decision-making processes necessary for problem-solving. Making all members of team feel valued and respected can help ensure that goals are met speedily and efficiently, undoubtedly leading to improvements in efficiency and performance, ultimately benefiting entire organization.

Seth Godin's exemplary skills as both an entrepreneur and intrapreneur demonstrate how vital of a skill it is for professionals in any industry to succeed - whether on their own or part larger organization. Also, the goal isn't just about completing tasks and achieving goals, but establishing meaningful connections that support the success *most* folks in the organization are trying to achieve.

16

Kutaragi

In the realm of technological advancement, a select few individuals have etched an enduring impact on the industry. Among this distinguished group lies Ken Kutaragi, renowned as the "Father of the PlayStation." Transitioning from a modest engineer to a trailblazing intrapreneur, Kutaragi's odyssey not only fuels inspiration but also imparts pivotal wisdom to budding entrepreneurs and aspiring business stalwarts.

At its core, Kutaragi's ascent embodies determination and unwavering commitment. With undying passion alight in his eyes, he envisioned revolutionizing gaming consoles; transcending mere entertainment into an immersive experience capable of captivating millions across the globe. Bearing witness to his resolute mindset is both awe-inspiring and powerful. Kutaragi's journey underscores profound lessons for those embarking upon entrepreneurial endeavors or taking charge in corporate landscapes alike.

First, it reminds us that innovation thrives when bold ideas are fearlessly pursued without hesitation or restraint. By daringly venturing into uncharted territories – combining cutting-edge technology with gaming tropes – Kutaragi reshaped perceptions and redefined boundaries within established industries.

Strategic collaboration emerged as integral throughout Kutaragi's voyages. Recognizing that transforming groundbreaking concepts into tangible products required cross-disciplinary expertise amalgamated through teamwork, he forged alliances with diverse professionals hailing from engineering to marketing disciplines,resulting in synergistic triumphs.

Noteworthy too is how resilience intertwines itself within every juncture of the Japan-born entrepreneur's legacy. Facing imminent adversity — including internal skepticism towards his radical visions —Kutargi powerfully persevered past initial setbacks while shielding an indomitable spirit against any notion of surrender. From these arduous experiences arises shared empathy for all who face doubt amidst their own quests for success—empathy fueling fortitude even during storms of discouragement.

Lastly, Kutaragi's tireless pursuit of excellence inspires individuals to remain discerning in their approach — avoiding complacency and challenging prevailing norms. His example reminds us to go beyond the facile, to envision not only how things are but also how they could be. Without Kutaragi's inventiveness, the world may have never witnessed the seismic evolution inherent in interactive entertainment, and millions would still reside firmly entrenched on this precipice of crappy animation, hungering for those engaging memories that only innovation can breathe life into.

Ken Kutaragi emerges as a luminary figure, encapsulating the spirit of technological ingenuity coupled with unwavering determination. Through his arduous journey from being a humble engineer to becoming an influential intrapreneur, he gave a few great lessons for aspiring entrepreneurs and leaders today: persist relentlessly amidst challenges; foster symbiotic collaborations; embrace a daring pursuit of innovation while shattering the confines of comfort. Ultimately, it is this resilient crusade against mediocrity that distinguishes extraordinary minds such as Kutaragi's- forging legacies that reverberate far beyond one individual's achievements.

V

What makes you tick?

"Just knowing you don't have the answers is a recipe for humility, openness, acceptance, forgiveness, and an eagerness to learn – and those are all good things."
Dick Van Dyke

17

Vested

It was day one.

I followed the tan-walled cubicles and grey carpet to my new workspace. I set my bag down at my assigned desk and began to reflect.

I had decided to leave my last gig because they weren't willing to change. To me, work was more than a 'job'. A job is somewhere I would punch-in and punch-out. I decided a long time ago that kind of work wasn't for me.

I knew that if I wanted to make it through the day, not dreading my time there, not watching the seconds tick by, not feeling resentful of every time I was pushed around or flat-out bullied by someone with a real confidence problem, I was going to need to be vested. I realized that if I became vested in an organization and that if my presence made an impact on the wins they accomplished, I was more likely to put up with the late hours, irritable coworkers and frankly, *confusing* customers.

In my heart, I knew what I was looking for. I was looking to lean into an organization and adopt its missions as my own. I was looking for an atmosphere where I didn't need to be told what to do next. I was looking for a challenge, and to be empowered with the feeling that I was going to find a way to do it.

In my heart I felt that If I owned the problem, then I could own the solution. It was quickly evident to me that owning that solution and seeing it come to fruition felt GOOD. Sure, the accolades and atta'boys gave me a brief smile, but there was something more.

However, *day one* at a new company is about learning the language. It's about learning who the stakeholders are and what drives every person you're going to be working with, reporting to, or avoiding. It was time for me to start there.

Learning the language

As a marketing and communications professional, I realized that my skills could be reapplied to almost any industry. The tactics shift, but the hard skills stayed the same. But also, as a marketing and communications professional, if I planned on convincing the customer my team knew what we're talking about, I had better learn it. This was something I would greet by diving into the industry the organization worked in.

To me, learning the language of an industry infers to more than just deciphering unique jargon or phrases abundantly used in a specific professional space. To gain proficiency in this specialized language opens up deeper understanding— as if discovering a new culture— plunging into its idioms, phrases and norms primarily embedded within the industry dynamics.

And within my first few years of practicing professional communications, I came to realize that virtually every field has its own peculiar lexicon; expressions camouflaged as ordinary speak, nevertheless exhibiting profound meanings beneath the facade to those agile enough to comprehend. Ranging from technical terminologies, coded speech, vital acronyms, to everyday jargon— every coinage essentially becomes a crucial stepping stone towards grasping such special language.

My first eye-opening moment here was also the most hilarious example in my repertoire. I was at my first BIG company. It was a *financial services* (not a 'bank'... see?) company in the northeast. I was working in a corporate communications role and assisting a team in rolling out new risk management policies, then driving and tracking adoption across the organization.

While interviewing some of the policy leaders at an oversized conference table on the gazillionth floor of a downtown high rise, I opened with the line, "So basically guys, why should folks want to adopt this new policy?"

"Well Chris" replied a bright young woman I often worked with, "it's basically our answer to socks. It's that easy. No?"

I looked around. I wasn't the youngest at the table. I wasn't the greenest. I wasn't the newest at the company. There were a handful of interns and a few associates who joined our meeting. I knew I wasn't the only one who had NO CLUE what the hell she meant.

I offered my apology. "I'm so sorry, I feel like I should know what you mean. But I've got to be missing something... Socks?"

"The Sarbanes-Oxley Act" she replied with a smile.

No, she wasn't talking about Chicago's less successful baseball team, but rather the compelling Sarbanes-Oxley Act of 2002—riveting stuff here.

Cue dramatic music...

In a nutshell, Congress set the stage post-Enron era and created this epic regulatory law called SOX, named after the the sponsors of the aforementioned bill. SOX attempts to protect innocent investors by forbidding banks from acting as rowdy teenagers nosing through personal diaries.

Rather than sneaking around with flashlight-in-mouth like amateur detectives hunting for accounting artifacts or information mummies, these banks are mandated to be forthcoming about their financial company skeletons thanks to this piece of legislation.

This act is further distinguished by something known as "internal controls," or—and let me simplify—steps designed to prevent bankers from accidentally "misplacing" a couple of billion dollars they had just last Tuesday.

About one week later, I had already sent a draft of my communication plan out to the folks I had met with. I was getting feedback from the same policy leaders to make sure what I was putting out on the company intranet was in fact true.

Since I had always told these folks to try and get to the point in any communication, they offered a perspective.

"I think you can cut this sentence down a bit. If you say SOX, everyone should know what you mean." the young lady from before suggested.

I rebuttled, "I'm sure most will! But, to be honest, I didn't. And being this company has A LOT of folks in it, not all being educated in financial legislation, we can't expect that the bank tellers who we're asking to make changes will know as well."

Light bulbs went off around the room. That was the moment that I realized that there is power in gathering outside perspectives. Sometimes we're too close to our projects. Sometimes part of knowing the language of an industry is understanding the different dialects as well.

What do the manufacturers call it?

What do the engineers call it?

What do the customers call it?

Each may have a different way of describing and perceiving the concept or idea you're trying to plan around. By understanding those dialects, you will be able to effectively communicate and drive the change you're looking to make in an organization.

Going beyond literally acquiring this linguistic competence

though is what seems most beneficial in understanding the 'feel' or essence of an industry. Essentially, it's immersing oneself into how these words and phrases are being lived out on a day-to-day basis; observing how a lingo shapes behaviors and decision patterns reflective of the industry standards.

Idioms

The role I reflected on above also gave me insight on "corporate speak".

Knowing that "blue-sky thinking" is corporate speak for "innovative ideas" is one thing but seeing it inform creatives' brainstorming sessions can help to connect certain concepts with concrete applications born from extensively-used expressions.

Importantly too - understanding such language unlocks new-found respect for storytelling within one's professional arena. Capturing years of shared experiences transformed into workplace discourse that pulsates among its experienced practitioners.

Flexibility also comes with learning an industry's discourse; well-equipped professionals stop at mere direct translation favoring an effortless transposition between their fields' vocabulary and rolling off conventional talk when communicating across different disciplines or industries.

Essentially, specialized linguistics and jargon special to different industries is similar to learning multiple human languages.

Like the difference between languages, which have distinctive vocabulary, grammar and syntax, various industries have advanced their own respective languages complete with unique terminology and technical jargon. The relationship between different languages and specialized professional vocabulary emphasizes the importance of being able to adapt linguistically and comprehend as well as express oneself in different professional environments.

For example, for individuals operating in the field of technology, familiarity with terms such as algorithms, coding languages and software architecture is necessary. Without such expertise, comprehension of technological advancements and meaningful conversation within the field would be quite a challenge. In the field of medicine, an extensive range of medical terminology exists which includes items such as diagnoses, procedures and pharmaceuticals. Such knowledge is required as a prerequisite to ensure safe and effective communication when attending to patients.

Just as different languages naturally evolve over time, language used in various industries is ever-changing. With each new technology come new terms. At the same time, terms formerly-known may fall into obsolescence. An individual working in a field must then adapt by continuously educating themselves and keeping up to date as new developments emerge.

Much like learning any new language, understanding industry-specific linguistics and jargon consists of more than simply memorizing terms. It entails the understanding of principles and concepts underlying industry-specific languages. In the legal field, being familiar with the legal language by no means indicates understanding law; a precise and sophisticated comprehension of legal systems, cases and civil and criminal procedures is necessary. In finance, being well-versed in financial jargon versus grasping theories of economics, investing and the functioning of financial markets is a distinctive difference.

To possess the ability to seamlessly switch from one industry language to another fuels growth in a professional manner, and it also fosters collaboration and innovation. In the same way someone who is multilingual is capable of overcoming cultural barriers and partaking in communication with people internationally, an individual fluent in industry-specialized linguistics has the ability to connect a multitude of areas of study and improve collaboration between professionals from different academic studies. A person's ability to speak multiple industry languages allows for the injection of novel perspectives, bridging of ideas and involvements between industries that at first would not appear to have much in common.

Having the necessary skills to maneuver and communicate across various industries sharpens skills and extends an individual's potential for professional growth. A philosophical professor may say something like, "The intrinsic act of speaking languages opens doors that lead to the flexibility to innovate and improve...."

In short, if you can learn the lingo from multiple industries, you will have the most powerful tool in the room, no matter your level of experience; **Perspective.**

18

Motivation & Frustration

One secret to a great job... one you actually like... one that has you working late because you're inspired, not because you have to... is to understand your work team. Not your boss. Not your subordinates. The people you work alongside.

Your frustration level will be cut in half when you understand what motivates your peer in the cubicle next to you. With this knowledge, you can tailor your approaches and language to suit your coworkers' motivational styles, thereby cutting down on misunderstandings and enhancing people's experiences within your work group. The same understanding will boost your ability to collaborate with colleagues in your organization in general, even those far beyond your work team.

To begin with, understanding your peers, and hence appreciating their perspectives, is critically important. Everyone is motivated differently: for some, recognition is paramount; for others, personal growth, while others crave money. Knowing why your colleague behaves the way she does and why she ranks her priorities in the way she does is the first step toward exercising empathy and patience when her behavior doesn't line up with your expectations. Remember that these motivational drivers represent people's most critical sense of well-being, so people's motivation will differ not just at work but throughout their lives.

Secondly, understanding your work team's peers can enable you to provide the support others need to rise to the occasion and excel. After all, if you understand why a particular peer is driven, you can ensure that he or she gets what she needs. If a coworker craves personal growth, make sure she gets opportunities for skill development and challenging projects. You will be helping her accomplish her professional goals but also contributing to his or her success and thereby the work team's. Take a proactive approach and offer this support before conflict and frustration crop up when the expectations of a coworker are not met.

Tailoring your communication style to suit others' motivational drives improves collaboration. Some people react best to the direct and forthright approach; others prefer a more inclusive, collaborative approach. Once you know what drives your co-workers, you are in a better position to engage them in open, productive dialogue–the better to minimize frustration that arises from misunderstandings. And the smoother collaboration process will follow.

Let's look at a fictional tech start-up in which a highly creative, intrapreneurial-minded Sarah is eager to make an impact.

Sarah strongly believes that working with people to develop

new ideas is more powerful than coming up with ideas as singulars. When Sarah meets a co-worker, Alex, who has been underestimated by most and has yet to be given a real creative challenge, she knows she has a chance to create an ally and a player who can help the tech start-up deliver amazing results. Most importantly, Sarah knows she can also set the stage for other players on the team to have the energy and fire to drive future projects forward - maybe at a time when Sarah can't exert the extra energy or oversight.

She sets a coffee date with Alex one week. They talk about the project and how including Alex in it would improve the project results. Sarah let Alex know that she didn't just want him on the team to say she was being "inclusive", but that she actually valued their input on what direction the project should take.

In Alex's eagerness, he flat-out tells Sarah that he is really excited to work with her on this project. Their conversation starts to escalate further and further into healthy debates and Sarah ensures to stress that this project isn't just about the results, but also it's to improve the teamwork environment. Sarah suggests that the team be introduced to weekly lunch and brainstorming sessions where every single team member participates and shares their own ideas. The more angles the project can be approached from, the better.

Once everyone started to see how Sarah and Alex began working together, a sense of healthy competition broke out. The team was no longer subdued by invisible barriers and the fear of sharing their ideas. Sarah opened the door to *intrapreneurship* by including Alex on the project. Archetypes are very typical but nevertheless need collaborative partners.

Understanding your peers can help you to identify opportunities for synergy. If you appreciate the diversity of strengths and motivation within your team, you can use those differences to build a stronger team. Internally assign complementary roles on the work team and communicate to people while thinking of the roles they play, their strong suits and motivational drivers. This will build a team that both values the members' contributions but engages each person fully.

When people know **why** they are doing something and are allowed to apply their **strengths**, they experience far less frustration.

19

You don't have to be the boss.

Leadership today is a fluid concept. Being the boss, holding the title, or being at the top of a group doesn't mean you make things happen or that you drive results. Sometimes, leadership means working to meet your group somewhere in the middle. Whether you are building consensus or rallying a team to beat a deadline or reach a goal, the real currency is your ability to collaborate and influence others.

In our fast-paced and competitive world, leadership is often associated with a title or a position of authority. However, being the boss or the leader on a team isn't the only way change gets made or productivity skyrockets. Change and results can actually happen faster and better if the team works collectively and has effective communication strategies.

First, it's important to remember the basis of any successful project: teamwork. By working with others, you are able to pool together the strengths and knowledge of individuals with different expertise to find unique solutions to complex problems.

Each person brings unique skills to the table that are different than those of other teammates. With some good balance and leadership, the team's strengths are activated, and results are reached much quicker.

Additionally, effective communication plays a major role in driving change and seeing results in a team. With open communication channels in place, ideas, concerns, and criticism can be voiced by each member. Listening to what others think can be crucial when making important decisions. In addition, having all needed information about a project will reduce confusion and result in a more productive outcome.

Last, being the leader on a team may not also mean having a fancy title next to your name. Leadership is the ability to influence others, inspire them to take action, and guide them to a specific goal. By taking the initiative on a team, being excited about the project, modeling a good work ethic and proactively helping set team and project goals, you can set a great example for the rest of your team. Taking initiative often sets an example that others are likely to follow even if they are at a lower role. Ask about other perspectives and provide yours when the team dialogue requires it.

You don't have to be the boss to make changes and get results. With the ability to work together and having effective communication strategies, individuals are able to participate and contribute to change and results. Being a boss might put you at the top position, however if you as the leader do not work well with others, you know won't be the boss for much longer. Teamwork and open communication promote a cohesive team that can work together and inspire others. Leadership does not hold a title but a mindset and actions done by anyone willing to help make things happen.

20

In parting...

As we wrap things up here, I have a few final thoughts. The phrase "We've always done it that way" should serve as a rallying cry for all those inspired to embrace intrapreneurship and effect change in their organizations. Intrapreneurs who challenge the status quo, and whose organizations have created an environment enabling them to do so, will change the world. In doing so, they will change not just the way we conduct business, but the very definition of success.

Remember this:

The path from dreamer to doer is often a long and tortuous one, lined with skeptics and often met with resistance. But in the end, the most powerful weapon you have in your arsenal is your unrelenting desire to make it different. Venture forth, armed with the knowledge and introspection that this book attempts to impart, and spark the change every organization so desperately needs.

Embrace intrapreneurship. And let's together shape a future where "We've always done it that way" becomes a testament to the boundless possibility of human imagination, the ruthlessness with which we write our own corporate script, and the power of progress.

Thanks for hanging out.
  Chris

About the Author

Christopher Novak, hailing from the charming city of Pittsburgh, Pennsylvania, is a marketing professional who possesses an impressive set of skills. Renowned for his quick wit and innovative problem-solving abilities, he has cemented his reputation as a true asset in the field.

A resident of the Steel City for years, Christopher Novak has honed his expertise through hands-on experience and unwavering dedication to excellence. His journey began with a passion for understanding consumer behavior, gradually developing into an indomitable prowess in strategic marketing.

What sets Christopher apart is not only his profound curiosity but also his innate ability to think outside the box. His clever insights and imaginative ideas harmoniously blend with tactical execution to yield remarkable outcomes. Adept at connecting intricate dots into cohesive strategies, he consistently astonishes colleagues and clients alike.

Moreover, Christopher's relentless dedication to delivering optimal results strengthens his standing as a true professional. Whether tackling intricate challenges or identifying untapped market potential, he remains resolute in ensuring that no stone is left unturned. This commitment transcends mere job requirements; it echoes throughout every aspect of his work ethic.

In addition to being highly skilled within the realm of marketing strategy implementation, Christopher carries himself confidently. Despite achieving numerous accolades throughout his career spanned several years now—each compliment entailing well-deserved praise—he remains grounded and focused on continual growth.

While some may view words like "witty" or "problem-solving" as disposable buzzwords within resumes or bios—the fleeting jargon employed by all-too-many individuals—Christopher embodies their definition sincerely. In him lies both intellectual curiosity intertwined effortlessly with interpersonal acumen—a balance that few can masterfully achieve.

www.ingramcontent.com/pod-product-compliance
Lightning Source LLC
Chambersburg PA
CBHW031301130726
47988CB00007B/2675